Body Fuel for Healthy Bodies
Fruits, Vegetables, and Legumes

Trisha Sertori

Marshall Cavendish
Benchmark

New York

This edition first published in 2009 in the United States of America by Marshall Cavendish Benchmark.

Marshall Cavendish Benchmark
99 White Plains Road
Tarrytown, NY 10591
www.marshallcavendish.us

First published in 2008 by
macmillan education australia pty ltd
15–19 Claremont Street, South Yarra 3141

Visit our website at www.macmillan.com.au or go directly to www.macmillanlibrary.com.au

Associated companies and representatives throughout the world.

Copyright © Macmillan Education Australia 2008

Library of Congress Cataloging-in-Publication Data

Sertori, Trisha.
    Fruits, vegetables, and legumes / by Trisha Sertori.
        p. cm. — (Body fuel for healthy bodies)
    Includes index.
    ISBN 978-0-7614-3799-4
    1. Nutrition—Juvenile literature. 2. Food crops—Juvenile literature. I. Title.
    TX355.S423 2009
    613.2—dc22
                                                        2008026209

Edited by Margaret Maher
Text and cover design by Stella Vassiliou
Page layout by Stella Vassiliou
Photo research by Claire Francis
Illustrations by Toby Quarmby, Vishus Productions, pp. 4, 5; Jeff Lang and
    Stella Vassiliou, pp. 8, 9; all others by Stella Vassiliou.

Printed in the United States

Acknowledgments
The author and publishers are grateful to the following for permission to reproduce copyright material:

Cover and header photos courtesy of © iStockphoto.com (vegetables); © iStockphoto.com/Galina Barskaya (girl); © iStockphoto.com/Sandra Caldwell (basil); © iStockphoto.com/Jennifer Conner (berries); © iStockphoto.com/Heather Down (beans); © iStockphoto.com/Elena Moiseeva (cherry tomatoes); © iStockphoto.com/Kristian Sekulic (boy).

Photos courtesy of:
123RF/Paulo Cruz, 6 (beans); Artville/Burke Triolo Productions, 17 (fruit jars); © Jean-Michel Labat/Auscape International, 20; © Ed Wige/Auscape/ BSIP, 25 (bottom); BananaStock, 15 (bottom); BrandX Pictures, 28 (top right); © Artman/Dreamstime.com, 29 (salt); © Borut Gorenjak/Dreamstime.com, 22 (middle); © Alexey Khromushin/Dreamstime.com, 7 (top); © Didier Kobi/Dreamstime.com, 29 (black pepper); © Olga Lyubkina/Dreamstime.com, 29 (2nd bottom left); © Robyn Mackenzie/Dreamstime.com, 28 (bottom left); © Feng Yu/Dreamstime.com, 29 (3rd bottom right); Getty Images/Dorling Kindersley, 29 (bottom right); Rita Maas/Getty Images, 27 (bottom); © iStockphoto.com, 6 (sweet potato), 8, 9, 10 (top), 16 (left), 24, 29 (top left), 30; © iStockphoto.com/Cathleen Abers-Kimball, 19 (bottom); © iStockphoto.com/Michael Braun, 11 (top); © iStockphoto.com/Florea Marius Catalin, 28 (bottom right); © iStockphoto.com/Norman Chan, 17 (can), 29 (3rd bottom left); © iStockphoto.com/Andriy Doriy, 29 (3rd top left); © iStockphoto. com/Elena Elisseeva, 12 (middle); © iStockphoto.com/Ilya Genkin, 12 (bottom); © iStockphoto.com/Graeme Gilmour, 7 (bottom); © iStockphoto.com/ Joe Gough, 6 (lettuce); © iStockphoto.com/Michael Hill, 16 (right); © iStockphoto.com/Rafa Irusta, 17 (legumes); © iStockphoto.com/Michal Kowalski, 28 (top left); © iStockphoto.com/Philip Lange, 21; © iStockphoto.com/Heiko Potthoff, 18; © iStockphoto.com/Amanda Rohde, 6 (top); © iStockphoto. com/Malcolm Romain, 7 (middle); © iStockphoto.com/Olena Savytska, 7 (2nd bottom); © iStockphoto.com/Gleb Semenjuk, 12 (top); © iStockphoto. com/Suzannah Skelton, 29 (top right & 3rd top right); © iStockphoto.com/Arnaud Weisser, 7 (cut apricots); © iStockphoto.com/Jaroslaw Wojcik, 29 (2nd bottom right); PhotoDisc/Jules Frazier, 29 (2nd top left); PhotoDisc/PhotoLink, 7 (2nd top); PhotoDisc, 28 (middle right); Photolibrary/ABN Stock Images/Alamy, 26 (top); Photolibrary/John Bavosi/Science Photo Library, 13 (bottom);Photolibrary/Martin Brigdale, 22 (bottom); Photolibrary/ Steve Cohen, 16 (middle); Photolibrary/Michael Diggin/Alamy, 22 (top); Photolibrary © Eye-Stock/Alamy, 27 (top); Photolibrary/Foodpix, 14 (top); Photolibrary/Profimedia International/Alamy, 17 (frozen vegies); Photolibrary/Andre Seale/Alamy, 23 (middle); Photos.com, 29 (2nd top right); Trisha Sertori, 23 (top & bottom); © Lim Yong Hian/Shutterstock, 28 (middle left); Stella Vassiliou, 1, 3.

MyPyramid symbols courtesy of U.S. Department of Agriculture.

While every care has been taken to trace and acknowledge copyright, the publisher tenders their apologies for any accidental infringement where copyright has proved untraceable. Where the attempt has been unsuccessful, the publisher welcomes information that would redress the situation.

Disclaimer
The health information provided in this book is general and in no way represents advice to the reader. The author and publisher take no responsibility for individual health or dietary decisions made in response to information contained in this book.

1 3 5 6 4 2

Contents

Glossary Words

When a word is printed in **bold**, you can look up its meaning in the Glossary on page 31.

What Is Body Fuel?

Body fuel is the energy, vitamins, and minerals we need to live. Just as cars need gasoline and computers need electricity, people need energy, vitamins, and minerals to work.

The best way to fuel our bodies is with a **balanced diet**. A balanced diet gives us all the **nutrients** our bodies need.

Nutrients in Foods

The nutrients in foods are divided into macronutrients and micronutrients.

Macronutrients provide energy. They are proteins, carbohydrates, and fats and oils. Micronutrients help **chemical reactions** take place in the body. They are vitamins and minerals.

The Food Pyramid

The food pyramid lists foods for healthy bodies. The colors shown (from left to right) are for grains, vegetables, fruit, oils, dairy, and meat and beans.

MyPyramid.gov
STEPS TO A HEALTHIER YOU

Fruits, Vegetables, and Legumes

Fruits, vegetables, and legumes are rich in micronutrients. These are the vitamins and minerals that cause many chemical reactions in the body. These foods are also a great source of fiber, which keeps the digestive system healthy. Thousands of different types of fruits and vegetables are grown around the world.

The Food Pyramid

Fruits and vegetables are found in the green and red parts of the food pyramid. Legumes are in the purple part of the pyramid. People need to eat lots of fruits and vegetables each day. This ensures the body has a steady supply of vitamins, minerals, and fiber.

Fruit Group
Focus on fruits

MyPyramid.gov

Vegetable Group
Vary your veggies

MyPyramid.gov

Meat & Bean Group
Go lean with protein

MyPyramid.gov

What Types of Fruits, Vegetables, and Legumes Are There?

People all over the world depend on fruits, vegetables, and legumes for their micronutrients, fiber, and carbohydrates. In some countries, people still gather their fruits and vegetables from wild plants. In other countries, these foods are grown on farms or in gardens at home.

Vitamin- and Mineral-rich Vegetables

There are hundreds of vegetables filled with fiber, vitamins, and minerals. Some of these are tomatoes, mushrooms, green leafy vegetables (such as lettuce), artichokes, sweet potatoes, peppers, and cucumbers.

Some types of vegetables are root vegetables, leafy vegetables, and seed vegetables.

Root Vegetables

Root vegetables are the roots of plants called tubers, such as potatoes.

Leafy Vegetables

Leafy vegetables are the leaves of plants, such as lettuce, that people eat.

Seed Vegetables

Seed vegetables are the seeds of plants, such as beans, that people eat.

Pome Fruits

Pome fruits have a fleshy edible fruit surrounding central seeds. Some pome fruits are apples, quinces, and pears. The most common pome fruits are apples. There are many different types of apples. They are grown in orchards in cool-climate countries around the world. Apples can be eaten raw or cooked as a dessert. Apple sauce is sometimes served with some pork dishes.

Citrus Fruits

Citrus fruits are fruits with a high **citric acid** content, such as oranges, lemons, limes, and grapefruit. Citrus fruits taste tangy and are full of vitamin C.

Tropical Fruits

Bananas, papayas, mangoes, and pineapples are common tropical fruits. These fruits grow in hot, humid climates and provide lots of fiber.

Stone Fruits

Peaches, nectarines, apricots, and plums are examples of stone fruits. They are called stone fruits because they contain a large, single seed. Stone fruits are seasonal. This means the fruit is only ripe at a certain time of the year.

Legumes

Legumes are high-protein beans. They can be eaten fresh, but are often dried. Legumes are the edible seeds of a variety of bean plants. They are often cooked in soups, made into dips, or cooked with meats. Some legumes are chickpeas, black-eyed peas, kidney beans, and lentils.

The Digestive System

The digestive system breaks down the foods we eat so they are ready to be absorbed into the bloodstream. Each part of the digestive system plays a part in breaking down, or digesting, foods. **Saliva** and **digestive enzymes** prepare to digest foods even before we eat them. They are produced when we see or smell foods.

Mouth
Teeth cut and grind food into smaller pieces. The enzymes in saliva start to break down carbohydrates in the food. The chewed food becomes a **bolus**, which is pushed down the throat by the tongue when we swallow.

Liver
The liver filters nutrients from the blood. Nutrients are sent to the small intestine for digestion. Waste is sent to the large intestine.

Gallbladder
The gallbladder stores bile, which is a digestive liquid made by the liver. Bile is used in the small intestine to break down fats.

Small Intestine
The small intestine is almost 23 feet (7 meters) long. Foods are digested in the small intestine after they are broken down in the stomach. Most nutrients are absorbed into our bloodstream through **villi** in the small intestine.

Esophagus
The bolus travels down the esophagus (ee-*soff*-a-gus) to the stomach.

Stomach
Stomach muscles churn the bolus. Acid in the stomach makes the food watery.

Pancreas
The pancreas makes enzymes that break down macronutrients.

Large Intestine
The large intestine is 5 feet (1.5 meters) long. It carries waste to the **rectum** for **evacuation** as **feces** (*fee*-seas).

Fabulous Body Fuel Fact

A bolus takes about three seconds to reach your stomach after it is swallowed.

How Does the Body Digest Fruits, Vegetables, and Legumes?

Digestion begins in the mouth. The body digests carbohydrates in fruits, vegetables, and legumes with an enzyme called amylase (*am*-il-ays). Amylase is released in saliva and in the small intestine. It breaks down carbohydrates so they can be absorbed.

Fiber

The fiber in fruits, vegetables, and legumes cannot be digested by humans. However, it is still important because it helps the body remove waste. Fiber is only found in plant foods.

There are two kinds of fiber, called **soluble fiber** and **insoluble fiber**. Soluble fiber becomes a thick gel in the digestive system. It slows the digestion of foods.

In the large intestine, insoluble fiber grows healthy **bacteria** that help to release the remaining nutrients from food. Insoluble fiber also acts like a broom. It sweeps waste along the large intestine for evacuation.

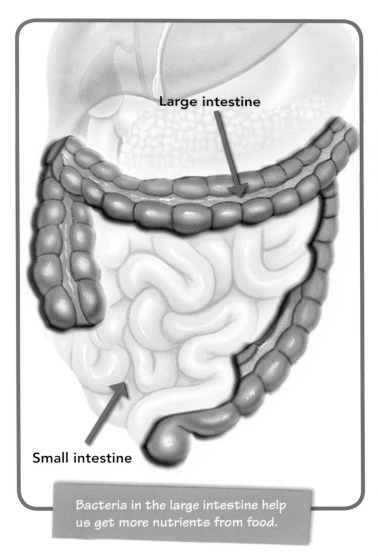

Large intestine

Small intestine

Bacteria in the large intestine help us get more nutrients from food.

How Does the Digestive System Absorb Fruits, Vegetables, and Legumes?

Nutrients in fruits, vegetables, and legumes are absorbed into the bloodstream from the small intestine. The carbohydrates in fruits are sugars called fructose (*frook*-tose) and sucrose (*sue*-croze). Fructose and sucrose are rapidly absorbed into the bloodstream through the villi. The bloodstream then transports these nutrients to every **cell** in the body.

Fiber for Extra Energy

Fiber slows the digestion of foods. This allows more nutrients to be absorbed from the small intestine and used for energy. Fiber also helps with the digestion of food in the large intestine. This releases even more nutrients for absorption.

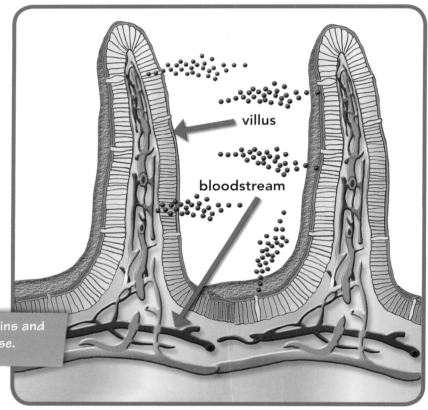

villus

bloodstream

Villi in the small intestine absorb vitamins and minerals as well as fructose and sucrose.

Body Fuel Health Tips

Fruits are high in sugars, such as sucrose and fructose. These sugars are easily absorbed and burn in the body as carbohydrate energy. Soluble fiber in fruit slows the absorption of these sugars. This means you get healthy, sustained energy.

How Do Fruits, Vegetables, and Legumes Help the Body Function?

Many fruits, vegetables, and legumes are high in carbohydrates, with lots of vitamins and minerals. These provide the body with energy. Most vitamins in fruits and vegetables are **water soluble** and leave the body in urine.

Using Energy

Some vitamins and minerals in fruits, vegetables, and legumes help the body use energy from macronutrients. The B-group vitamins thiamine and riboflavin help break down carbohydrates. This helps the body use energy from the carbohydrates in fruits, vegetables, and legumes.

Vitamins and minerals help the body obtain the energy needed for exercise.

Body Fuel Health Tips

If you eat different fruits and vegetables, you get a bigger range of important nutrients. One example is the **phytochemicals** in citrus fruit. Phytochemicals are the **antioxidants** in fruit and vegetables. Add fruit to your day, and get those antioxidants to work.

What Nutrients Are in Fruits, Vegetables, and Legumes?

Different fruits, vegetables, and legumes have different nutrients. Legumes, some fruits, and root vegetables have a high **starch** or sugar content. These fruits and vegetables have lots of carbohydrate energy and fiber. Other fruits and vegetables, such as spinach, have lots of fiber and micronutrients such as iron.

The different colors of fruits and vegetables are often a key to their nutrients. For example, red fruits and vegetables often have lots of vitamin C. Green vegetables have lots of iron. Choosing different-colored fruits, vegetables, and legumes delivers lots of different vitamins and minerals.

Nutrients in Fruits, Vegetables, and Legumes			
Nutrients	**Fruits**	**Vegetables**	**Legumes**
Macronutrients			
carbohydrate	•	•	•
protein	•	•	•
fats and oils			•
Micronutrients			
Vitamins			
vitamin A	•	•	
vitamin B1			•
vitamin B2	•	•	
vitamin B3	•	•	•
vitamin B5	•	•	
vitamin B6	•		•
vitamin B9	•	•	•
vitamin C	•	•	
vitamin E	•		
vitamin K		•	
Minerals			
calcium	•	•	•
iron		•	
magnesium	•	•	•
molybdenum			•
phosphorous	•	•	
potassium	•	•	
selenium	•	•	

You can eat different-colored fruits, vegetables, and legumes to get different nutrients.

How Does the Body Use These Nutrients?

Nutrients from food are used in many ways in the human body. Carbohydrates are used for energy. Vitamins and minerals are used in chemical reactions in the body.

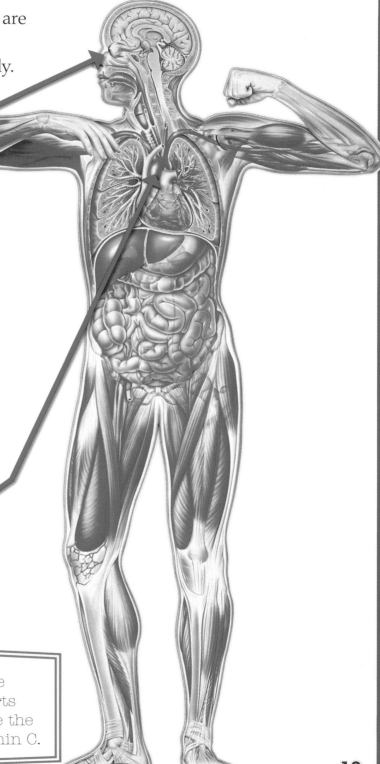

Eyesight
Sweet potatoes and carrots are packed with beta carotene, which changes into vitamin A in the body. Vitamin A is essential for healthy eyesight and healthy cell growth.

Blood Clotting
The blood contains special substances that allow it to **clot**. Vitamin K, found in probiotic yogurt, green vegetables, and soybeans, helps to maintain these substances.

Healthy Cells
Many fruits and some vegetables have lots of vitamin C. Vitamin C helps keep cells healthy and protects them from damage.

Red Blood Cells
Green leafy vegetables have the B-group vitamin pyridoxine (*pii*-rid-*ox*-in). Pyridoxine is used in human growth and red blood cell function. Red blood cells carry oxygen in the bloodstream.

Fabulous Body Fuel Fact

Some Indigenous Australians harvest the tiny bush tomato that grows in the deserts of northern Australia. Bush tomatoes are the size of a fingernail and have lots of vitamin C.

13

Fueling the Body with Fruits, Vegetables, and Legumes

Carbohydrates are the main body fuel in fruits, vegetables, and legumes. This comes from the starch in legumes and in vegetables such as potatoes and yams. Legumes also have lots of protein. Fruit has carbohydrates in the form of sugar. The fat in most fruits, vegetables, and legumes is low or zero. However, many fruits and vegetables are mainly eaten for their micronutrients and fiber.

Obesity

Obesity is when people are very overweight. It is usually caused by eating too much food and getting too little exercise. Eating plenty of fruits and vegetables can reduce the risk of obesity.

People can maintain a healthy weight more easily when they eat less fat. Replacing fatty foods with fruits, vegetables, and legumes provides plenty of fiber. This makes the stomach feel full, so people eat less.

Preparing a salad is easy and provides lots of nutrients for body fuel.

Body Fuel Health Tips

Choose whole fruit instead of fruit juice. Fruit juice gives you less nutrition and fiber than a whole piece of fruit. It also has fewer nutrients and more sugar than a piece of fruit. This means you are likely to drink more energy than you need.

How Many Servings of Fruits, Vegetables, and Legumes Do I Need Daily?

Healthy adults need around 1,800 to 2,800 **calories** (7,500–11,500 kilojoules) daily. Almost half these calories should come from fruits, vegetables, legumes, and grains. People need two servings of fruit each day and at least five servings of vegetables.

Fruits

One serving of fruit could be:

- a piece of fruit, such as an apple
- a handful of grapes
- a handful of cherries
- 2 plums.

Vegetables and Legumes

Servings of some high-carbohydrate vegetables are:

- 1 cup of yams
- 1/2 cup of cooked corn
- 1 or 2 medium potatoes.

Servings of some high-fiber vegetables are:

- 1/2 cup of carrots
- 1 cup of fresh peas and beans
- 1/2 cup of cooked legumes, such as lentils.

Servings of some vegetables that are high in minerals and vitamins are:

- 1 cup of cooked spinach
- 1/2 cup of cooked mushrooms
- 1/2 cup of cooked broccoli.

Body Fuel Health Tips

Health bars, such as granola or yogurt bars, often have lots of added sugar and fats. They are usually not very healthy at all. The energy in an apple is around 48 kcal (200 kJ). If people replace a health bar with an apple they eat fewer kilojoules, have longer-lasting energy, and plenty of soluble fiber.

You can eat an apple to get one of your servings of fruit.

Healthy Food Choices

All fruits, vegetables, and legumes are healthy food choices. However, they can be less healthy when they are mixed with foods such as sugar or butter. Fruits, vegetables, and legumes can be eaten:

- raw
- steamed
- baked
- boiled
- stir-fried
- deep-fried
- roasted.

The following table shows some healthy ways to prepare and eat fruits, vegetables, and legumes.

✓ Healthy Choices	✗ Less Healthy Choices
Carbohydrate Vegetables, such as Potatoes, Yams, and Peas	
steamed, boiled, baked, mashed with low-fat milk and a dash of olive oil	deep-fried, mashed with butter and salt, roasted in animal fat
Other Hard Vegetables, such as Carrots, Turnips, and Beets	
steamed, raw, lightly boiled, stir-fried	roasted or fried in animal fat or butter
Green Vegetables, such as Spinach, Broccoli, and Peas	
raw, lightly steamed, stir-fried	over-boiled, with added butter and salt
Fruits	
fresh, dried, preserved without sugar	jams, juice, fruit bars, fruit cocktail, with sugar added
Legumes	
boiled, mashed into patties, added to soups	

Fabulous Body Fuel Fact

Some health bars have more saturated fat than fried bacon!

Fresh or steamed fruits and vegetables are healthier choices than fried foods, such as french fries.

Preserved Fruits, Vegetables, and Legumes

Fruits, vegetables, and legumes are often preserved. This means they are dried, cooked, or frozen so they can be stored for long periods. Preserving fruits, vegetables, and legumes by drying, bottling, freezing, or canning means these foods can be exported around the world. However, preserving can also add sugars to foods and reduce their micronutrient content.

Drying

Fruits and legumes are often dried. This preserves them for many years, and they retain fiber, protein, carbohydrates, vitamins, and minerals.

Bottling

The most common way people preserve fruits is by bottling them or making jam. The fruits are cooked and placed in glass jars. The jars are specially sealed and then heated to preserve the fruits.

Freezing

Vegetables are often frozen and can last for many months. Freezing does not reduce the vitamin and mineral content in vegetables.

Canning

Many fruits and vegetables are canned. Canning is similar to bottling. Foods are sealed inside the cans, which are then heated to cook the food.

Preserved fruits and vegetables can be kept for longer periods than fresh fruit and vegetables.

Body Fuel Health Tips

Most nutrients in fruits and vegetables are maintained when they are frozen, canned, or fresh. Cooking can reduce nutrients, so steam quickly to keep these nutrients.

Functional Foods

Many of the foods we eat each day are very good for us. Food scientists call them "functional foods." That is because these foods have ingredients that may improve health and reduce diseases.

Functional fruits, vegetables, and legumes have naturally occurring phytochemicals that may improve health. When people eat these foods they get the high food value of the foods plus added health benefits.

Phytochemicals

Phytochemicals are chemicals made by plants. Some phytochemicals can improve people's health. There are thousands of different types of phytochemicals that may help to prevent diseases. They can act as:

- antioxidants
- enzyme stimulators
- **DNA** protectors.

Antioxidant phytochemicals in citrus fruits, leeks, tomatoes, carrots, and onions may lower the risk of heart disease and cancers.

Enzyme-stimulating phytochemicals in cabbage, beans, citrus fruits, and cherries help enzymes work better. This may reduce the risk of cancers.

DNA-protecting phytochemicals in chili and beans keep DNA healthy.

Benefits from Phytochemicals

People receive the benefits of phytochemicals if they eat a variety of fruits and vegetables.

Cherries are delicious to eat and contain phytochemicals for extra health benefits.

Functional Foods Working Together

Many fruits, vegetables, and legumes are functional foods because of their high levels of micronutrients. When people eat these foods together, they often have extra health benefits.

Many of the chemical reactions that take place in the body may use more than one micronutrient. Vitamins and minerals may work together to improve their effect. Macronutrients, such as carbohydrates, may need micronutrients to start working.

Some examples of this are listed below.

- The riboflavin, or vitamin B2, in broccoli, mushrooms, and brussels sprouts helps convert carbohydrate to energy.

- The vitamin C in citrus fruits helps the body absorb the calcium in dairy foods.

Body Fuel Health Tips

People can help prevent disease by eating two pieces of fruit and five servings of vegetables a day. This is about 2-1/2 cups of vegetables a day. Eating a healthy diet rich in phytochemicals helps us stay healthy throughout life.

Many vegetables, such as mushrooms, contain micronutrients needed for health.

Naturally Healthy Fruits, Vegetables, and Legumes

Most fruits and vegetables are naturally rich in health-giving nutrients. Some are super-powered with antioxidants and omega-3 fatty acids.

Super Fruits and Vegetables

Some super-powered fruits and vegetables are:

- citrus fruits, which help keep skin soft and stretchy, and may reduce colds
- avocados, which promote healthy blood circulation
- brussels sprouts, which reduce the risk of cancers, help keep skin soft and stretchy, and help the **immune system**
- kiwis, which help control sugar levels in the blood and may relieve asthma
- green beans, which help build healthy bones, help in blood clotting, are **anti-inflammatory**, and may relieve asthma
- spinach, which may reduce the risk of cancer, is anti-inflammatory, and helps in blood clotting
- apples, which help relieve asthma and may also help lung function.

Vegetables that are fresh from a garden often have more nutrients than vegetables from a store.

Fabulous Body Fuel Fact

Some people use herbs and spices to treat their patients. Healers who use herbs are called herbalists.

What Are Herbs and Spices?

Herbs and spices come from plants. Herbs are usually made from leaves. Spices are made from roots, bark, buds, fruit, or seeds. Some herbs and spices are believed to have health benefits.

Spices

- Ginger may reduce travel sickness and may be an anti-inflammatory.

- Garlic may lower unhealthy fats in the blood and help relieve colds.

- Cloves are a natural painkiller.

- Cinnamon may help control levels of sugar in the blood.

Herbs

- Oregano may promote healthy lungs and relieve stomach upsets.

- Rosemary may reduce stomach upsets and can be rubbed on the skin to help soothe sore muscles.

- Thyme may help colds and can be used on cuts to help prevent infections.

- Fennel may clean the liver.

Try adding herbs and spices to meals for extra flavor and health.

There are many different herbs and spices to choose from.

Hot paprika · Smoky paprika · Sweet paprika · Ground chili · Moroccan spice · Grenada spice · Curry powder · Turmeric · Ground saffron · Vanilla beans

Cinnamon sticks · Ground ginger · Ginger roots · Chili · Cloves · Mustard grains · Sesame seeds · Aniseed · Ground cinnamon · Ground vanilla

Fruits, Vegetables, and Legumes Around the World

The types of fruits, vegetables, and legumes people eat depend on local climates. Countries with cool climates, such as Ireland, grow different types of plants than do tropical countries such as Indonesia or hot and arid countries such as Egypt.

Ireland

The Irish have grown potatoes as a staple crop for hundreds of years. The Irish have many ways to cook potatoes. One of them is a meal called boxty potatoes, where the potatoes are mixed with flour to make potato cakes.

Egypt

Dates are an important fruit in Egypt. They grow on palm trees and are believed to have been farmed for more than three thousand years.

India

Many Indian dishes are based on legumes, such as chickpeas and lentils. Lentils are boiled with herbs and spices to make a delicious dish called dhal. Dhal is eaten with flat Indian breads called roti and chapatti.

Fabulous body fuel fact

The potato was first introduced to Ireland in 1589 by the British explorer Sir Water Raleigh.

As you can see from this world map, people around the world eat lots of different types of fruits, vegetables, and legumes.

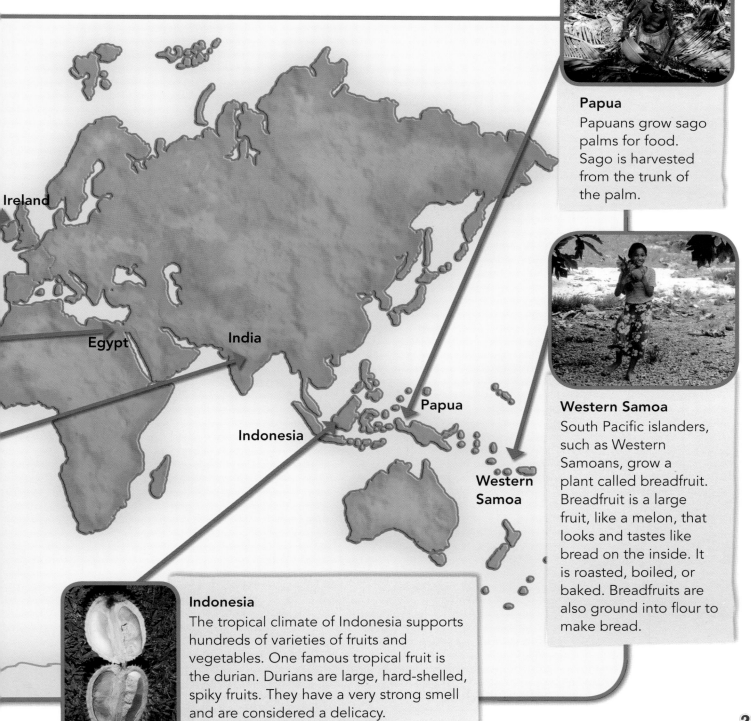

Papua
Papuans grow sago palms for food. Sago is harvested from the trunk of the palm.

Western Samoa
South Pacific islanders, such as Western Samoans, grow a plant called breadfruit. Breadfruit is a large fruit, like a melon, that looks and tastes like bread on the inside. It is roasted, boiled, or baked. Breadfruits are also ground into flour to make bread.

Indonesia
The tropical climate of Indonesia supports hundreds of varieties of fruits and vegetables. One famous tropical fruit is the durian. Durians are large, hard-shelled, spiky fruits. They have a very strong smell and are considered a delicacy.

Ireland

Egypt

India

Papua

Indonesia

Western Samoa

23

Allergies and Intolerances To Fruits, Vegetables, and Legumes

Food allergies and intolerances are reactions by our bodies to different foods. A food allergy occurs when the immune system reacts as if a food is dangerous. This reaction may cause itchy skin or make breathing difficult. A food intolerance is a negative chemical reaction in the body to a food. These reactions often cause similar symptoms to allergic reactions.

Chemical Intolerance

Chemicals, such as fertilizers and pesticides, are sometimes sprayed on crops as they are growing. Monosodium glutamate (MSG) is sprayed on some crops in the United States. Sulphur dioxide is added to some dried fruits and fresh vegetables and fruits. Chemicals such as these can sometimes cause allergic reactions.

Naturally Occurring Chemicals

Some fruits and vegetables have naturally occurring chemicals. This means the chemical is a natural part of the fruit or vegetable. Some naturally occurring chemicals that can cause allergies or food intolerance are:

- salicylates (sa-*liss*-a-lates), found in many fruits and vegetables, such as apples, tomatoes, and corn
- tyramine, found in avocados, eggplants, grapes, oranges, pineapples, plums, and the dried fruits prunes and raisins
- histamine, found in bananas, strawberries, and tomatoes.

Many farmers spray their crops with pesticides, which kill insects that eat the plants.

What Can I Eat if I Am Allergic to Some Fruits, Vegetables, and Legumes?

There are hundreds of fruits, vegetables, and legumes to choose from. This means that substituting allergy-producing fruits and vegetables with other foods is easy. First, it is important to discover what is causing the allergic reaction.

Elimination Diets

Doctors can test for allergies by placing people on elimination diets. These are very strict diets that have no allergy-producing foods. After two to four weeks, other foods are added to the diet. Doctors can check for reactions to see if these foods are the cause of the allergy.

Skin-scratch Test

Another allergy test is the skin-scratch test. Small amounts of allergy-producing ingredients are placed on the person's skin. If the person has reactions, such as itching or rashes, they are allergic to that ingredient.

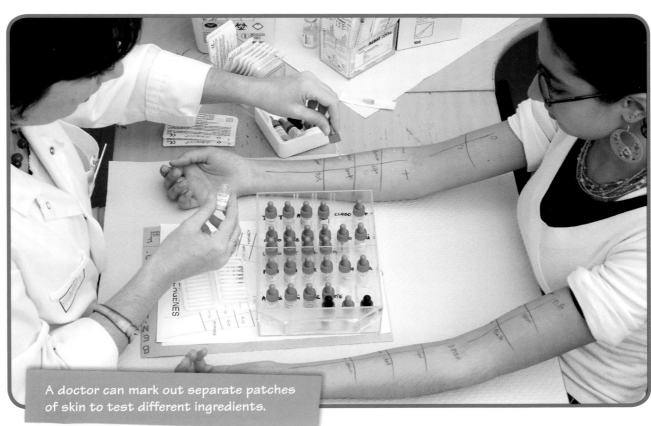

A doctor can mark out separate patches of skin to test different ingredients.

Checking Food Labels for Fruits, Vegetables, and Legumes

Some fruits, vegetables, and legumes are sold in cans or dried in packages with labels. Food labels can help people choose healthy foods. People can check labels to see if foods are organic, or if they have added sugars and fats.

Packaged foods have labels that list calories, salt, sugar, and preservatives in food. The labels also show:

- the name and address of the manufacturer
- a use-by date
- the weight of the food
- how the food was processed.

Check food labels on the following packaged fruits, vegetables, and legumes.

People can check signs and labels in stores to see if food is organic.

Foods	Ingredients to Check
Health bars and fruit bars	Choose foods with lots of fruit and less fat and sugar.
Jams	Choose jams with whole fruit, rather than fruit flavor.
Canned fruits and vegetables	Choose foods without added salt or sugar and fruits in natural juice, not syrup.
Fruit juices	Choose juices that are 100 percent fruit juice, without added sugar or preservatives.
Frozen vegetables	Choose products without salt or preservatives.
Dried fruits	Choose fruits without sulphur dioxide.

Fresh Fruits, Vegetables, and Legumes

Fresh fruits, vegetables, and legumes do not have food labels. People cannot tell what chemicals, pesticides, and fertilizers were used as the food was growing. Traces of some chemicals and fertilizers may be absorbed into the food as it grows.

Organic Foods

Many supermarkets, farmers' markets, and other natural food stores sell organic foods. These foods are grown without chemicals, such as pesticides or manufactured fertilizers. All organic foods must be certified by government officials before they can be labeled organic.

Soil Testing

To make sure organic foods have no added chemicals, government officers test soils at organic farms. If any chemical residue is found, the foods cannot be labeled organic.

Preserved fruits and vegetables, such as canned pears, have labels with information about the food.

A food label also provides information about the calories and nutrients in the food.

Fabulous Body Fuel Fact

Onions contain a gas that is released when the onion is cut. This gas reacts with the sticky fluid in the eye, causing it to sting and tear. Chill onions before cutting them to reduce the gas release.

Cooking Class

Ask an adult to help you.

Fruit salad and roasted vegetables are delicious and healthy. These recipes supply:

- carbohydrate for energy
- protein for cell renewal
- phytochemicals for healthy cells
- fiber for digestive health
- vitamin A for eyesight
- vitamin C for healthy skin and bones
- phosphorous for bones.

Five-minute Fruit Salad

Servings   Four
Preparation time   15 minutes

Ingredients

10 strawberries

1/2 pineapple

2 bananas

1/4 watermelon

2 peaches

juice of 2 oranges

Preparation

1. Chop all fruits into 1/2-inch (1-centimeter) cubes.
2. Mix in a large bowl.
3. Squeeze the orange juice over the top.
4. Mix and serve with low-fat yogurt or cottage cheese.

strawberries

watermelon

pineapple

peaches

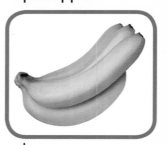
bananas

orange juice

Rainbow of Roasted Vegetables

Servings   Four to six
Preparation time   30 minutes
Cooking time   1 hour

Ingredients

1 large sweet potato, chopped into
    1-1/2-inch (4-centimeter) chunks

2 large red peppers, seeded and cut
    into quarters

3 large carrots, cut in half, then quartered

1 large zucchini, chopped into quarters

3 redskin potatoes, quartered

1 large red onion, cut into quarters

1 large yellow onion, cut into quarters

8 cloves of garlic, crushed

1/2 cup rosemary sprigs

4 tablespoons extra-virgin olive oil

pinch of salt

crushed black pepper

cooked couscous

Preparation

1. Preheat the oven to 450 degrees
   Fahrenheit (220 degrees Celsius).

2. Place the chopped vegetables, garlic,
   rosemary, and oil in a very large bowl.
   Add a pinch of salt and black pepper.

3. With clean hands, mix the vegetables
   and other ingredients, lightly coating
   the vegetables with olive oil.

4. Spread the vegetables in a large
   baking dish.

5. Roast in the oven for 40 to 50 minutes or
   until golden and soft.

6. Serve with couscous.

sweet potato

yellow onion

red peppers

garlic

carrots

rosemary sprigs

zucchini

olive oil

redskin potatoes

salt and pepper

red onion

cooked couscous

Fueling the Body with Healthy Fruits, Vegetables, and Legumes

Fruits, vegetables, and legumes deliver a supercharge of the micronutrients the body needs for health. Micronutrients are used in every part of the body, including cells, bones, and skin. Getting plenty of these foods is as easy as eating two pieces of fruit every day and five servings of vegetables.

Fruits, vegetables, and legumes come in a rainbow of colors. Mixing these colors on your plate makes all foods look appetizing. It also delivers nutrients that will keep you healthy and active for life. Eating lots of fruits, vegetables, and legumes provides great body fuel for healthy bodies.

Fresh fruits and vegetables taste good and are good for you.

Glossary

anti-inflammatory	reduces swelling
antioxidants	chemicals that protect cells from damage
bacteria	tiny living things that live in soil, water, plants, animals, and humans
balanced diet	a mix of different foods that provides the right amount of nutrients for the body
bolus	a small ball of chewed food
calories	units used to measure energy
cell	a microscopic structure that combines with other cells to make up all the bones, muscles, and other parts of the body
chemical reactions	processes by which substances are changed into other substances
citric acid	an acid found in tiny amounts in the cells of almost all living things
clot	harden to form a lump, such as a scab
digestive enzymes	proteins that speed up the chemical reactions involved in the digestion of food
DNA	the material that stores genetic information, such as hair and eye color (abbreviation of deoxyribonucleic acid)
evacuation	removal from the body
feces	solid waste that is evacuated from the body
immune system	the body system that fights infections
insoluble fiber	fiber that does not break down in water
nutrients	substances that provide energy when eaten
phytochemicals	chemicals made by plants
rectum	the end of the large intestine, where feces are stored before evacuation
saliva	the fluid in the mouth that helps digest food
soluble fiber	fiber that breaks down in water
starch	the carbohydrate found in root vegetables, such as potatoes
villi	small, fingerlike bumps on the inside wall of the small intestine
water soluble	can be dissolved in water

Index